FRANK MAHOVLICH

JOE PRIMEAU

CURTIS JOSEPH

DARRYL SITTLER

MATS SUNDIN

DAVE KEON

RICK VAIVE

DOUG GILMOUR

FRANK CLANCY

GRANT FUHR

DAVE WILLIAMS

ALEXANDER MOGILNY

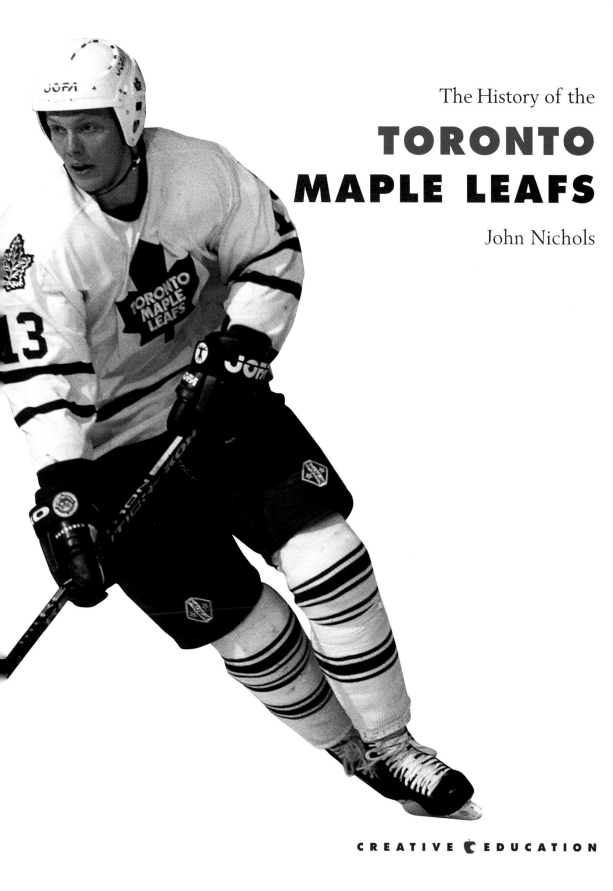

The History of the

TORONTO
MAPLE LEAFS

John Nichols

CREATIVE ⬤ EDUCATION

Published by Creative Education, 123 South Broad Street, Mankato, MN 56001

Creative Education is an imprint of The Creative Company.

Designed by Rita Marshall.

Photographs by Hockey Hall of Fame (Graphic Artists, Imperial Oil-Turofsky, London Life-Portnoy,

Doug MacLellan, Miles Nadal), Icon Sports Media Inc. (John Cordes), SportsChrome USA

(Gregg Forwerck, Craig Melvin, Bob Tringali)

Library of Congress Cataloging-in-Publication Data

Nichols, John, 1966– The history of the Toronto Maple Leafs / by John Nichols.

p. cm. — (Stanley Cup champions)   ISBN 1-58341-274-3

Summary: Presents the history, players, and accomplishments of the Toronto

Maple Leafs.

1. Toronto Maple Leafs (Hockey team)—History—Juvenile literature.

[1. Toronto Maple Leafs (Hockey team)—History. 2. Hockey—History.] I. Title. II. Series.

GV848.T6 N53 2003   796.962'64'09713541—dc21   2002034927

First Edition 9 8 7 6 5 4 3 2 1

TORONTO, ONTARIO, IS THE LARGEST CITY IN CANADA.
LOCATED ON THE WESTERN SHORES OF LAKE
ONTARIO, THE CITY IS THE CHIEF COMMUNICATIONS,
manufacturing, and financial center of Canada. Toronto is also home
to many cultural attractions, such as the Art Gallery of Ontario and
the Royal Ontario Museum. The city's towering skyline serves
notice that this is truly a modern metropolis.

The people of Toronto have many interests, but the sport of
hockey owns a special place in their hearts. For decades, the citizens
of Toronto have cheered for the team that wears the maple leaf
(Canada's national symbol) on its chest: the National Hockey
League's (NHL) Toronto Maple Leafs. And with one successful
decade after another, the Leafs have established themselves as one
of the most storied franchises in all of professional sports.

CONN SMYTHE

{EARLY GREATNESS} The early history of the Leafs is largely the story of one of the NHL's founding fathers: Conn Smythe.

Joe Primeau sparked the offense in the early **1930s**, leading the team in assists for five seasons.

Smythe, whose name is today found on the trophy honoring the top performer in the playoffs each year, bought a team called the Toronto St. Patricks in 1926. The St. Patricks were first organized in 1917 as an original member of the NHL, but after the purchase, Smythe promptly changed the club's name to the Maple Leafs.

The Maple Leafs were an average team during the late 1920s, but Smythe slowly added such talented players as center Joe Primeau and wings Charlie Conacher and Harvey "Busher" Jackson. On defense, Smythe acquired Hall-of-Famers Frank "King" Clancy and Clarence "Hap" Day to keep opposing offenses in check. By the 1931–32 season, the Maple Leafs were flying high, defeating the Chicago Blackhawks, Montreal Maroons, and New York Rangers in

CURTIS JOSEPH

Hap Day played 11 seasons for the Maple Leafs, then coached them for 10 seasons.

HAP DAY

the playoffs to claim the Stanley Cup—the big silver chalice awarded to the NHL champion.

The Maple Leafs remained competitive, but it was 10 years before they celebrated another championship. This time, coached by former player Hap Day, the Leafs won the Stanley Cup by doing something no team had done before or since. They rallied from a three-games-to-none deficit against the Detroit Red Wings to win four straight games and claim the 1942 title. "It's the most amazing thing I've ever been a part of," said winger Gordie Drillon. "We just wouldn't quit."

The Leafs won the Cup again in 1945 but missed the playoffs the next year. Looking at a team in decline, Smythe quickly rebuilt. Behind center Syl Apps, goaltender Walter "Turk" Broda, and defenseman Gus Mortson, the Maple Leafs stormed back to the top

Walter "Turk" Broda was awarded the Vezina Trophy (as the NHL's best goalie) in **1940–41**.

WALTER BRODA

From Gordie Drillon to Glenn Anderson, Toronto has featured many great wings.

GLENN ANDERSON

of the NHL. The new Toronto juggernaut captured four league championships in the five years between 1947 and 1951. Smythe proudly referred to the impressive Maple Leafs dynasty of the late 1940s and early '50s as "the greatest team I've ever had."

In one **1957** game, the Maple Leafs exploded for 14 goals in a 14–1 drubbing of the Rangers.

{THE LEAFS PACK A "PUNCH"} During the rest of the 1950s, Toronto remained a good but not great team. The Maple Leafs made trips to the Stanley Cup Finals in 1959 and 1960 but were turned away both times by their Canadian archrivals, the Montreal Canadiens. Looking for a way to take Toronto back to the top, Smythe turned the team over to veteran coach and general manager George "Punch" Imlach.

A native of Toronto, Imlach had a feisty attitude and a knack for building winners. He was rarely seen without his fedora hat, and his swollen nose revealed years of hockey-inflicted bumps and

FRANK MAHOVLICH

bruises. The new coach and general manager's first order of business

was to build a strong defense. He put Johnny Bower in goal and sta-

tioned Allan Stanley on defense. Then, on offense, Imlach assembled

an exciting mix of young talent and veteran savvy that included

wing Frank Mahovlich and centers Dave Keon and Bob Pulford.

Mahovlich and Keon were the jewels of this collection.

Mahovlich was a tall, graceful skater known throughout the league as the "Big M." He won the Calder Trophy in 1957–58 as the

league's Rookie of the Year and scored 48 goals in 1960–61. The 5-foot-9 and 165-pound Keon had a very different style. Zipping around the ice, the little center seemed to be everywhere at once. Constantly pestering bigger, slower opponents, Keon took a beating but never stopped charging the net. "Frank Mahovlich might have been the engine of the Leafs in the 1960s," Smythe was fond of saying, "but Davey Keon was our spark plug. Without him, the engine wouldn't run."

From 1962 to 1964, the Maple Leafs engine ran at high speed. Imlach's club captured three straight Stanley Cups, defeating Chicago once and Detroit twice. After losing to the eventual champion Montreal Canadiens in 1965 and 1966, the Leafs came roaring back

DAVE KEON

once more. Dubbed the "Over the Hill Gang" (Toronto's players

averaged more than 30 years of age), the Maple Leafs rode the hot

goaltending of Bower and Terry Sawchuk to a six-game series victory

over Montreal in 1967 to claim their 11th Stanley Cup.

{THE MAGNIFICENT SIX} The Leafs' 1967 Stanley Cup run

was the last for Imlach's aging Leafs. By 1970, the coach had left

Toronto to join the Buffalo Sabres, and most of the team's great

veterans had either retired or moved on to other teams.

The Toronto teams of the 1970s were competi-

tive and exciting but never quite good enough to

capture the Stanley Cup. During the 1970s and '80s,

the Maple Leafs were the property of Harold Ballard,

a colorful and eccentric owner whose penny-pinching

ways resulted in a long stretch of lean years.

Multitalented defenseman Borje Salming posted 620 career assists— the most in club history.

Although the Maple Leafs were less than championship-caliber,

they did have a core of players who were among the finest in the

NHL. Goalie Mike Palmateer, defensemen Ian Turnbull and Borje

Salming, wingers Lanny McDonald and Dave "Tiger" Williams, and

center Darryl Sittler came to be known as the "Magnificent Six"

among Toronto's hockey-crazy fans.

The 5-foot-9 and 170-pound Palmateer made up for his lack of

BORJE SALMING

With players such as **1990s** star Doug Gilmour, Toronto has captured 11 Stanley Cups.

size with great quickness. Salming was one of the great iron men of the NHL, playing 15 seasons in Toronto and setting the franchise

Darryl Sittler scored 18 career hat tricks (games with three or more goals) for the Maple Leafs.

record for assists with 620. Turnbull was a gifted offensive defenseman, netting 20 goals twice during his career with the Leafs. McDonald scored 35 or more goals four times in seven Toronto seasons, and tough guy Williams finished his career as the NHL's all-time leader in penalty minutes.

But of all the Leafs stars of the 1970s, Sittler shined the brightest. The 6-foot and 190-pound native of Kitschner, Ontario, had a deft scoring touch, netting 389 goals and totaling 916 points (goals plus assists) in 12 seasons with the Maple Leafs. A great leader, Sittler succeeded Dave Keon as Toronto's captain in 1975 and wore the captain's "C" for the next six seasons.

Sittler provided what may have been the Maple Leafs' finest

DARRYL SITTLER

moment of the '70s on February 6, 1976, when he scored six goals

and added four assists in an 11–4 victory over the Boston Bruins.

The amazing 10-point game shattered the previous record of eight

held by Montreal's Maurice "Rocket" Richard and Bert Olmstead. "It

was one of those nights where everything I touched went in or went

over to somebody else who scored," recalled Sittler.

{VAIVE KEEPS HOPE ALIVE} The Maple Leafs continued

their stumbling ways during the 1980s, as Ballard's frugal ownership

style kept the franchise stuck in a rut. Frustrated by

the team's mismanagement, Sittler frequently

quarreled with the front office and was eventually

traded to the Philadelphia Flyers. Without its franchise

player, Toronto dropped to fifth place in the Norris

Division standings in 1981–82.

Fortunately for long-suffering Leafs fans, the team still had a

number of other players capable of generating excitement.

Defenseman Al Iafrate and wings Gary Leeman and Wendel Clark

all gave some impressive performances during the dry spell.

But perhaps Toronto's brightest star of the '80s was Rick Vaive.

The 180-pound winger turned heads when he scored 33 goals

during his first full season in 1980–81. Vaive was just getting started,

DAVE WILLIAMS

WENDEL CLARK

Wendel Clark spent 13 seasons with the Maple Leafs, three of them as team captain.

however. Over the next three seasons, he netted 54, 51, and 52

goals, becoming the first Maple Leafs player ever to "light the lamp"

50 times in a season.

Vaive scored most of his goals by outfighting

opposing defensemen for loose pucks in front of the

net. He also possessed an extremely hard and accurate

slap shot. Without much of a supporting cast around

With his knack for scoring, Rick Vaive was one of the NHL's brightest stars in the early **'80s**.

him, Vaive was often the focus of opposing teams' entire defensive

gameplans. Opponents tried to slow Vaive down by punishing him

with body checks and challenging him to fights. Although not par-

ticularly big, Vaive answered all challenges. "Rick is one tough guy,"

said Leafs defenseman Bob McGill. "A lot of guys thought they

could take him. A lot of guys were wrong."

The Maple Leafs' best seasons of the 1980s were 1985–86 and

1986–87. Toronto qualified for the playoffs both seasons and won

RICK VAIVE

its first-round series before being eliminated by the St. Louis Blues

and Detroit Red Wings, respectively.

{GOOD-BYE TO THE GARDEN} Despite his management

failings, the death of Harold Ballard in 1990 shook the Toronto

franchise. After his passing, the team went through a series of legal

power struggles that weren't resolved until businessman Steve Stavro assumed ownership of the team in 1994.

By then, though, the Leafs were well on their way to recovery.

In 1991, Toronto hired Cliff Fletcher as its president

and general manager. Known as the "Silver Fox" due to

his gray hair and sharp hockey mind, Fletcher immedi-

ately began revamping the team. Trades for veteran

All-Stars such as winger Glenn Anderson, center Doug

Gilmour, and goalie Grant Fuhr added winning savvy to a team

comprised mainly of young players.

> Wing Dave Andreychuk topped the hallowed 50-goal mark in both **1992–93** and **1993–94**.

The Leafs immediately began to improve. In 1992–93,

Toronto posted its first winning record in 13 years. Midseason

acquisition Dave Andreychuk pumped in 25 goals in 31 games, and

Gilmour racked up 127 total points as Toronto made the playoffs.

The rising Leafs then beat the Detroit Red Wings and St. Louis

Blues in back-to-back seven-game series before falling to the Los

D. ANDREYCHUK

Angeles Kings in yet another seven-game thriller.

Toronto returned to the Western Conference Finals the follow-

Toronto sent four players to the **1994** NHL All-Star Game, including goaltender Felix Potvin. ing year but came up short again, this time losing to the Vancouver Canucks. Despite the loss, the Leafs were back among the league's elite teams, and Toronto fans were once again roaring their approval at Maple Leaf Gardens—the team's home since 1931.

As the decade wore on, the Leafs featured some new stars. Goalie Curtis Joseph, known to fans as "Cujo," came over as a free agent in 1998 and immediately gave the team a new swagger. High-scoring center Mats Sundin became the Leafs' captain in 1997 and then posted three straight seasons of 30 or more goals. In 1999, Toronto made another strong playoff run, defeating the Philadelphia Flyers and Pittsburgh Penguins before losing to the Buffalo Sabres.

After the 1999 playoffs, the Maple Leafs closed one chapter in

FELIX POTVIN

their history and started another. The team moved out of Maple Leaf Gardens and into the brand-new Air Canada Centre—a state-of-the-art arena with room for 19,000 fans. "This is a beautiful building," said Sundin. "But I think we will all leave a little piece of ourselves at the Garden."

{A NEW TRADITION} In 1999–00, with the help of new wing Gary Roberts, the Maple Leafs went 45–30–7 and captured the Northeast Division title. The next season, Toronto continued to rise as young players such as wing Darcy Tucker began to show their potential.

Before the 2001–02 season, Toronto added offensive punch by signing talented wing Alexander Mogilny. Mogilny and Sundin combined to score 65 goals as Toronto made the playoffs again. In the first two rounds, the Leafs battled past the New York Islanders and Ottawa Senators in a pair of marathon seven-game series. In the

Veteran wing Gary Roberts was the NHL's sharpest shooter in **2000–01**, scoring on 29 of 137 shots.

GARY ROBERTS

Always ready for a fight, wing Tie Domi was one of hockey's toughest players.

TIE DOMI

Combining rare size, speed, and instincts, Mats Sundin had the Leafs on the rise.

MATS SUNDIN

conference finals, the tired Toronto lineup fought hard but fell to

the Carolina Hurricanes in six games. "It's the hardest championship

to win in sports," said Gary Roberts. "This time just

wasn't our time."

Toronto fans looked for big things from 6-foot-6 and 220-pound wing Nikolai Antropov.

After the season, Curtis Joseph left town as a free

agent, but the Leafs quickly replaced him with anoth-

er All-Star goalie: veteran Ed Belfour. Belfour gave the

Leafs a proven netminder with a champion's resume, having led the

Dallas Stars to the 1999 Stanley Cup.

The Toronto Maple Leafs' history, covering nearly eight

decades, includes some of the highest highs and lowest lows the

game has seen. Through it all, the Leafs have been backed by some

of the NHL's most loyal and passionate fans. Today, the men who

wear the symbol of Canada proudly upon their chests stand ready

to add another chapter to Toronto's winning tradition.

N. ANTROPOV